D0741973

Butler Children's
Collection Fund

of the Library Foundation

Generous gifts to

The
Library
FOUNDATION

further the work of Multnomah County Library

Walruses

by **Renee C. Rebman**

Marshall Cavendish
Benchmark
New York

Special thanks to Donald E. Moore III, associate director of animal care at the Smithsonian Institution's National Zoo, for his expert reading of this manuscript

Copyright © 2012 Marshall Cavendish Corporation

Published by Marshall Cavendish Benchmark
An imprint of Marshall Cavendish Corporation

All rights reserved. No part of this publication may be reproduced, stored in a retrieval system or transmitted, in any form or by any means, electronic, mechanical, photocopying, recording, or otherwise, without the prior permission of the copyright owner. Request for permission should be addressed to the Publisher, Marshall Cavendish Corporation, 99 White Plains Road, Tarrytown, NY 10591. Tel: (914) 332-8888, fax: (914) 332-1888. Website: www.marshallcavendish.us

This publication represents the opinions and views of the author based on Renee C. Rebman's personal experience, knowledge, and research. The information in this book serves as a general guide only. The author and publisher have used their best efforts in preparing this book and disclaim liability rising directly and indirectly from the use and application of this book.

Other Marshall Cavendish Offices:
Marshall Cavendish International (Asia) Private Limited, 1 New Industrial Road, Singapore 536196 • Marshall Cavendish International (Thailand) Co Ltd. 253 Asoke, 12th Flr, Sukhumvit 21 Road, Klongtoey Nua, Wattana, Bangkok 10110, Thailand • Marshall Cavendish (Malaysia) Sdn Bhd, Times Subang, Lot 46, Subang Hi-Tech Industrial Park, Batu Tiga, 40000 Shah Alam, Selangor Darul Ehsan, Malaysia

Marshall Cavendish is a trademark of Times Publishing Limited

All websites were available and accurate when this book was sent to press.

Library of Congress Cataloging-in-Publication Data
Rebman, Renee C., 1961-
Walruses / by Renee C. Rebman.
p. cm. — (Animals animals)
Includes index.
ISBN 978-0-7614-4881-5 (print)
ISBN 978-1-60870-622-8 (ebook)
1. Walrus—Juvenile literature. I. Title.
QL737.P62R427 2012
599.79'9—dc22
2010016036

Photo research by Joan Meisel

Cover photo: Paul Nicklen/Getty Images

The photographs in this book are used by permission and through the courtesy of:
Alamy: Jim Corwin, 7; Arcticphoto, 12, 15, 39; Louise Murray, 23; Andrew Woodward, 32; Interfoto, 37; Peter Arnold, Inc., 41. *Corbis*: Paul Souders, 24. *Getty Images*: 11; Paul Oomen, 1; Thomas Kitchin & Victoria Hurst, 8; Paul Nicklen, 9, 17, 18; Darrell Gulin,19; Norbert Rosing, 26, 30; National Geographic, 29; Daisy Gilardini, 34; *Glow Images*: Stock Connection, 20. *Peter Arnold, Inc.*: Andrew Stewart/SpecialistStock, 4

Editor: Joy Bean
Publisher: Michelle Bisson
Art Director: Anahid Hamparian
Series Designer: Adam Mietlowski

Printed in Malaysia (T)
1 3 5 6 4 2

Contents

Marine Mammals

The hungry walrus glides through the icy ocean water. While swimming, its huge body is both graceful and powerful. It dives to the bottom of the seafloor to search for food. After feeding, it surfaces and swims to an ice *floe*. The walrus plunges its long white *tusks* into the ice and gets a good grip. Attached to the floe, it floats quietly in the water for a short while. Then, using its strong *flippers*, the walrus hauls its awkwardly shaped body on top of the floe. It stretches out next to another walrus, turns its face to the sun, and rests.

The scientific family name for a walrus is Odobenidae. This is a Greek term meaning "tooth walker." The walrus does not use its tusks to walk but

A walrus will take a break from swimming by resting on an ice floe.

does use them for many tasks, and they are one of its most distinct features.

The name "walrus" comes from the old Scandinavian word *valroos*, which means "whale-horse". It is believed this word dates back to the Vikings, who traveled the seas and probably saw many valroos on their voyages. The sailors may have been combining names of two large animals in describing the walrus because it is so big.

There are actually two different types of walruses, the Pacific and the Atlantic. They are named after the oceans where they make their homes. The Pacific walrus is larger than the Atlantic walrus.

Pacific walruses live in the Bering seas and in other parts of the Pacific and Arctic oceans between Russia and Alaska. Atlantic walruses live along the coasts of Greenland and northeastern Canada in the Atlantic and Arctic seas. In these areas the temperature is between 5 degrees Fahrenheit (-15 degrees Celsius) and 41 °F (5 °C). Both types *migrate* southward in the winter when the waters get covered by heavy ice. They return to the northern areas of the oceans as the ice retreats in the spring. These yearly migrations cover around 2,000 miles (3,219 kilometers).

Walruses enjoy being in the water, even when the waters in which they swim are frigid cold.

There are an estimated 200,000 Pacific walruses. There are about 20,000 Atlantic walruses. Because they live in different oceans, the two types of walruses never see each other. Both need the frigid ocean waters to survive. It is the source of all of their food.

Walruses are marine *mammals*. They spend about two-thirds of their time in the water. These animals

Species Chart

◆ An adult male Pacific walrus can weigh as much as 3,800 pounds (1,724 kilograms) and measure 9 to 12 feet (3 to 4 meters) in length. Females can weigh up to 2,800 pounds (1,270 kg) and are 7 to 10 feet (2 to 3 m) long.

A Pacific walrus.

◆ An adult male Atlantic walrus can weigh as much as 1,900 pounds (900 kg) and measure 9.5 feet (3 m) in length. Females can weigh up to 1,200 pounds (560 kg) and measure 8 feet (2 m) long.

breathe oxygen and give birth to live young. They are warm–blooded. This means their internal body temperature remains constant. Their amazing bodies keep them warm no matter how cold the weather is.

Because walruses live in such cold climates, scientists have difficulty studying them. Walruses are social with one another but avoid other animals and people. Walruses in the wild immediately retreat when they see or smell a human.

Much of what we know about the walrus has been learned from the walruses kept in captivity in zoos. These highly intelligent animals do well in captivity and are a favorite among zoo guests. Walruses are often featured in shows that display their natural behaviors as they interact with their trainers. These sessions keep the animal both mentally and physically active.

Did You Know . . .
Walruses are exceeded in size by only one other *pinniped*—elephant seals. These are odd-looking creatures. The males have a big proboscis (nose) that looks a little like a short elephant trunk. Male elephant seals are 16 feet (5 m) long and weigh 6,000 pounds (2,722 kg).

A trainer at the New York Aquarium gets affectionate with a walrus.
It takes a lot of time and patience to gain the trust of a walrus.

2 Flippers, Tusks, and Blubber

At first glance, a walrus appears to be a large, awkward animal with funny whiskers and long white tusks. But each of these features serves an important purpose.

Walruses are a cinnamon brown color, although young walruses can be a dark brown. Their skin is tough and leathery and is covered in short hairs. Like many mammals and other animals, the walrus will *molt* (lose its hair) each summer, then hair will grow back. This seasonal molt is similar to birds losing their feathers.

Their skin is about 1 inch (2 centimeters) thick. The males have many bumps called *tubercles* around their neck and shoulders. Underneath the skin is a

Walruses are instantly recognizable because of their long tusks.

thick, 6-inch (15 cm) layer of *blubber* that keeps the walrus warm. About one-third of its total body weight is body fat. Having tough skin also protects walruses from most *predators*.

Walruses are one of three kinds of pinnipeds, which are animals that have fins or flippers as their limbs. The other two types of pinnipeds are seals and sea lions. Seals cannot walk with their flippers. Instead, they must flop along on their bellies. Both walruses and sea lions are able to walk on all four flippers. On land, a walrus can walk as fast as a human.

The skin on the underside of each walrus flipper is rough, giving the flippers traction on the ice. The flippers also have five bony digits with webbing between each one. Each digit ends in a very small claw. The walrus uses its hind flippers to swim, and steers with its front flippers.

Walruses are excellent swimmers. They usually cruise along at a rate of 4 to 6 miles (6 to 10 km) per hour, but can reach 20 miles (32 km) per hour. When diving, a walrus will usually stay underwater for around ten minutes but can stay under for up to thirty minutes, if necessary. Their incredible lungs and

This close-up look at a walrus flipper shows webbed digits with a claw on the end of each one.

strong flippers mean walruses can dive deep. Although they usually stay in shallow waters not exceeding 300 feet (91 m), they can easily accomplish a dive to 600 feet (183 m).

The walrus is perhaps best known for its two long white tusks and bushy whiskers, giving it an appearance of a toothy old man with a mustache. The tusks are made of *ivory* and begin to grow when the walrus is about eighteen months old. They will continue to grow throughout the walrus's life. A male walrus has longer tusks than a female—about 40 inches (102 cm) long. The female's tusks will reach about 30 inches (76 cm) in length.

Did You Know . . .

When a walrus swims in the frigid sea, its blood vessels constrict and its color fades to a pale gray. When the animal gets out of the water, its blood flow returns and its body changes back to its usual pinkish-brown color.

The tusks serve many useful purposes. Walruses use them to grab on to ice floes and to chop breathing holes in the ice. They also use them to defend themselves against predators or during fights with other walruses. Tusks are also important to help the walrus stir up food along the bottom of the ocean. Males will often display their tusks by throwing back their heads to prove their dominance. The male with the longest tusks usually wins the role of dominant male of a group. Sometimes a tusk will wear down or break off. Tusks do not grow back, and this does not hurt the animal, although a male will lose his rank within his group if his tusks do break off.

The walrus has cheek teeth inside its mouth, which are used for crushing shells during eating. They are always growing. In fact, the teeth have growth rings inside just like the growth rings inside of a tree trunk. Each year as the teeth grow, another ring appears. By examining a cheek tooth, the age of a walrus can be determined.

A walrus has an incredible amount of whiskers, usually four to seven hundred

arranged in thirteen to fifteen rows on the snout around the mouth. These are called *vibrissae*, and they are extremely sensitive. If anything brushes against the vibrissae, even underwater, the walrus feels it immediately. Walruses depend on their vibrissae even more than their eyes. The animal has tiny eyes and poor eyesight.

These adult walruses have varying sizes of tusks.

Walruses try to show their dominance by displaying their tusks to other walruses.

On top of the vibrissae are two small nostrils. Scent helps a walrus recognize other walruses. Mother walruses use scent to identify their babies. A walrus will also pick up the scent of a nearby predator and be able to alert other walruses.

Their hearing is excellent, even though they have no external ears, just flat openings in their skin. Walruses can hear one another from more than a mile away. They communicate by bellowing, barking, growling, whistling, clacking their tusks, and making other sounds. They can make sounds both above and below the water.

The walrus has a small, square, powerful skull. Underwater, a walrus can use it like a sledgehammer to break through ice several inches thick. This awkward, blubbery mammal is built to survive in the harsh conditions of frigid ocean waters.

A close look at a walrus's nostrils and whiskers.

3 Daily Life Of a Walrus

Walruses do not like to be alone. They are social animals and live in large *herds* with up to two thousand members. Socialization is extremely important to the walrus. Walrus herds stay together all year around. Females herd with other females and young walruses. Mature males stay together in all-male herds. They only seek out females during mating season.

There is a social order in each herd. Each walrus has its place. The leaders are the largest members with the biggest tusks. Leaders are also louder and more aggressive than the other members. When a walrus flings back its head and points its tusk at another member, it means "get out of my way." It may also roar and make loud noises to intimidate another walrus.

A herd of walruses rests in the water at a sanctuary in Alaska.

For the most part, walruses get along and enjoy being together. Their favorite activity is resting together on a *haulout*. A haulout is the name for any place where walruses gather, usually on a large ice floe. A herd prefers to rest on a free-floating ice floe so water is available on all sides. The ice must be thick enough to support their collective weight and large enough for the herd. If no ice is available, the herd will go to the shore. They always remain close to the water. A herd will return to a favorite haulout over and over again.

When a herd is resting together, there is a tangle of walruses. Some snuggle side to side, some stretch out on their backs, and some even lie on top of other walruses. The members seem to enjoy the closeness. The close contact means shared body heat that will help keep them warm in frigid conditions. But even in mild weather herd members pile up against one another.

Gathering in a herd means members have some protection from predators. Walruses look out for one another. If one senses danger, it will sound the alarm to the herd with a loud barking noise. A huge stampede into the water follows.

Did You Know . . .

Walruses have a built-in flotation device. They can suck air into special air sacs in their necks. These keep the animals' heads above water, and they can float in an upright position. Walruses easily sleep while floating and even *nurse* their young while vertical. The *calves* hang upside down in the water while nursing.

Walruses gather close together for companionship and warmth.

While a walrus spends much of its time resting on a haulout, it spends most of its day swimming in the water and searching for food.

The walrus is a *carnivore*. This means it eats meat. A walrus's diet consists mostly of small sea creatures, such as mollusks and clams, which are soft-bodied creatures with hard shells. They also eat crustaceans, which have external skeletons, such as shrimp and crabs. Worms, sea stars, and sea cucumbers are also in their diet. These main food sources of the walrus all live on the bottom of the sea. Occasionally some walruses will eat seals or, if food is scarce, birds.

To find food, the walrus dives to the floor of the ocean. Although it can make deep dives, it prefers to hunt in shallow waters less than 150 feet (46 m) deep. Walruses hunt for food twice a day. They have to dive many times to find enough food for each meal. Most dives last several minutes in length. The walrus comes to the surface to catch its breath and rest for a few minutes between dives.

Once the walrus reaches the ocean floor, it roots through the gravel with its snout. It pushes itself forward with its hind flippers and drags its tusks through the sediment. Deep under the water, the

A walrus swims underwater in search of food.

walrus has very little visibility. It relies on its vibrissae to feel for prey. The sensitive whiskers detect the slightest movement. Once food is found, the walrus takes it directly into its mouth. If the prey is buried under sand, the walrus sucks water into its mouth, then shoots a stream into the sand to blast away the sand to reveal the prey.

Walruses do not use their cheek teeth to chew their food, instead they swallow it whole. If the animal has a shell, the walrus cracks or crushes the shell with its cheek teeth, then sucks out the animal and swallows it. An adult walrus can consume three to six thousand clams during a single feeding. It takes a lot of food to fill up such a large animal. Walruses need to eat about 6 percent of their body weight daily. This is around 180 pounds (82 kg) of food. A pregnant walrus increases that amount by another 30 to 40 percent, or around 250 pounds (113 kg) of food a day.

Swimming, hunting for food, and resting on a haulout with its herd make up the daily life of a walrus.

4 The Life Cycle Of a Walrus

Walruses are good mothers. Each knows which calf is hers and keeps it nearby. Females are quick to help any calf in danger or to retrieve one that strays. Every walrus born has many older females to look out for it.

A female walrus (also called a cow) is not ready to mate until she is around six years old. Mating season occurs from January to March. During this time, females looking to mate separate themselves from other females and form a separate herd. Not all females mate every season, as some may already be pregnant.

A male walrus is mature at around eight to ten years of age but probably will not mate until he is closer to fifteen years old. During mating season, one

A female Atlantic walrus and her infant rest on an ice floe.

or more large adult males (also called bulls) spend time around the female herd when searching for a mate. Only a few of the most dominant males are present. Less dominant and immature males remain in an all-male herd.

The males make many different sounds to attract the attention of the females, including whistling and clacking their teeth. They also use the air sacs at the back of their throats to produce a deep bell-like sound. Although walruses are generally nonviolent, during mating fierce fighting sometimes breaks out between competing males. They attack, using their tusks to slash at each other. Older males often have many scars on their leathery skin due to these fights.

Females usually pick the largest, most mature bulls that make the loudest sounds and dominate the fighting. Once a female is interested in a certain male, the two walruses swim far away from the herd to mate in the water. After mating, the female rejoins the herd. The male will most likely return to the herd and mate with many different females. Once mating season is over, males leave the females and live with their own herd.

When a female walrus has chosen a mate, the two will swim off together to mate.

The *gestation* period for a walrus is fifteen months. There is a period of delayed implantation. This means the fertilized egg floats in the mother's uterus without attaching for four to five months. Then it will attach to the uterine wall and begin to develop. This delay serves two purposes. It ensures that the birth will occur during warmer weather when the calf will have the best chance for survival. It also

A walrus reassures her calf with a tusk rub and flipper hug.

gives the mother's body a rest in case she is still caring for another young calf. Walruses give birth every two years.

Calves are born on sea ice. Walruses give birth to only one calf at a time and twins are extremely rare. The newborn calves measure around 4 feet (1 m) in length and weigh 120 to 140 pounds (54.4 to 64 kg). They are completely dependent on their mother for food and safety. The mother is very protective of her calf and often shields it between her two front flippers to keep it safe on crowded ice floes. Females with newborns will form a separate nursing herd. Nursing herds can have from twenty to two hundred members.

Walruses are attentive, loving, and caring toward their young. They have been observed playing with their offspring. The calves crawl over their mother's backs, and the mothers sometimes lift them up into the air with their front flippers.

Calves begin to swim very early—within two weeks of birth. If they become tired, they hitch a ride on their mother's back.

Did You Know . . .

On a haulout, the most dominant males get the best spots. They take their place in the center of the floe, and the younger males surround them. If a predator threatens the pack, the walruses retreat into the water and swim quickly away with the most dominant male in the lead.

A mother walrus will stick close by her calf for some time after giving birth.

Calves do not have a large amount of blubber and get cold easily, so they usually do not stay in the water for too long. If they get cold, they simply return to the ice and snuggle against their mother. If a mother leaves her calf to search for food, the other females watch over it.

A mother walrus will nurse her young for about one year. Calves begin to supplement their diet with solid food at about six months. Calves grow quickly and gain about 2 pounds (1 kg) per day. Even after nursing stops completely, a calf will remain with its mother for at least two years. If the mother does not become pregnant again, the calf may stay with her even longer. If the calf is a bull, it will eventually leave to join an all-male herd. Female calves will become independent but will stay within their mother's herd for life. A healthy walrus can live up to forty years.

5 A Protected Species

Even with their massive size, walruses have some natural predators. Killer whales and polar bears hunt them. Full-grown adult walruses will fight back, slashing their opponents with their powerful tusks. But younger and weaker walruses are occasionally killed by these predators.

Humans, however, are their most fierce predators. Humans have hunted walruses for centuries. Native peoples of the northern regions surrounding the Atlantic and Pacific oceans hunt walruses to survive. They use the meat for food and other parts of the walrus to make useful and necessary items. No part of the animal is wasted.

The polar bear is one of the walrus's greatest predators.

The Inuits live along northern sea coasts of Canada, the United States, Russia, and Greenland. They have hunted walruses for 4,500 years. Hunting walruses is a big part of their tradition and is crucial to their way of life. The Inuits use walrus intestines for raincoats and stretch them out for window coverings. The skin is used as clothing, and the ivory tusks are used to make jewelry or are carved with fine decorative pictures known as *scrimshaw*. Walrus oil is used to cook food and fuel lamps. Bones are used to make spearheads, and large rib bones are used in the making of boats.

One type of Inuit boat is called an umiak. This boat is framed in wood and is about 20 to 30 feet (9 to 12 m) in length. It sometimes has a sail that can be fitted on a removable mast. Walrus and seal skins are tanned and oiled to make them waterproof and then they are stretched over the framing. Umiaks are sometimes called women's boats, as women and children ride in them during voyages while men paddle kayaks alongside. Umiaks are also used during hunting and whaling expeditions as well as for trading, since the boats are capable of transporting heavy loads.

The ivory from walrus tusks has been used for many purposes for many years. This sculpture is from the twelfth century.

Native peoples use the skin from walruses to build boats called umiaks.

For a long time, only native peoples hunted walruses. But commercial hunting began during the 1600s. Walrus oil and walruses' beautiful ivory tusks were much in demand. Thousands of walrus were killed every year. By the 1800s the animal had been hunted to near *extinction*.

Use of fossil fuels, such as coal, became popular, and the demand for oil produced by the walrus dropped off. Various protective laws also came into being, both nationally and internationally. Gradually, walrus populations began to grow again.

Global warming is a big problem for arctic animals. The natural *habitat* of the walrus is becoming diminished. Changing weather conditions means fewer ice floes are present. There are fewer available for haulouts. When haulouts become overcrowded, young calves accidentally get crushed to death.

While walruses are not currently in danger of becoming extinct, they are a protected species. This means their population

Did You Know . . .
The Congressional Walrus Act of 1941 banned all commercial hunting of the animal in U.S. waters. The U.S. Marine Mammal Protection Act of 1972 made it illegal to hunt any marine mammal in U.S. waters. It is still legal to keep walruses for scientific study.

is being closely watched. Only natives are allowed to hunt walruses for personal use. Inuits and other native peoples do not kill enough walruses to seriously threaten their population. It is estimated they kill around six thousand walruses per year.

Controversy over protecting the walrus still continues. On February 8, 2008, the Center for Biological Diversity filed a petition to list the Pacific walrus as threatened or endangered under the Endangered Species Act. The petition states global warming threatens the walruses' habitat and decreases the availability of the animals' prey. It also states that without sea ice the walruses will be forced into a shore-based existence to which they have not adapted.

This petition will lead the way for more studies to be conducted and heighten awareness of the problem of losing the sea ice habitat. Many organizations around the world are concerned about the welfare and survival of walruses. Hopefully, with help, walruses will be around for a long time, and many generations to come will be able to enjoy these amazing giants of the sea.

Global warming puts walruses in danger. If the ice floes on which they rest melt, the walruses will have nowhere to go to rest, and they will drown.

Glossary

blubber—A thick layer of fat that lies just underneath the skin.

calves—Baby walruses.

carnivore—An animal that feeds on animal flesh, meat eating.

extinction—No longer existing.

flipper—A flat limb with bones that helps the walrus swim and walk.

floe—A flat mass of floating ice.

gestation—Pregnancy.

habitat—The place or environment where an animal lives.

haulout—A place where walruses gather out of the water.

herd—A group of animals of one kind.

ivory—Hard white material that makes up the tusk of a walrus.

mammal—A warm-blooded animal; female mammals feed milk to their young.

migrate—To move from one place to another to feed or breed.

molting—The annual shedding of hair.

nurse—The act of young getting milk from its mother.

pinniped—A seal, walrus, or sea lion with flippers.

predator—An animal that hunts and kills another animal for food.

scrimshaw—A carved or engraved article made from ivory.

tubercles—Large bumps found on the skin of the walrus around the neck and shoulders.

tusk—One of a pair of very long front teeth.

vibrissae—The sensitive whiskers on a walrus's snout.

Find Out More

Books

Miller, Connie Colwell. *Walruses*. Mankato, Minnesota: Capstone Press, 2006.

Miller, Sara Swan. *Walruses of the Arctic* (Brr! Polar Animals). New York: PowerKids Press, 2009.

Rake, Jody Sullivan. *Walruses*. Mankato, Minnesota: Capstone Press, 2007.

Weber, Valerie, *Walruses* (Animals That Live in the Ocean). New York: Gareth Stevens, 2008.

Websites

Alaska Sealife Center
www.alaskasealife.org

Arctic Studies Center
www.mnh.si.edu/arctic/html/walrus.html

Canadian Museum of Nature
www.nature.ca/notebooks/english/walrus.htm

Sea World Education Department
www.seaworld.org/infobooks/walrus/home.html

Walrus Facts and Information
www.walrus-world.com

Index

Page numbers for illustrations are in **boldface**.

About the Author

Renee C. Rebman has published more than a dozen nonfiction books for young readers. Her Marshall Cavendish titles include *Anteaters*, *Turtles and Tortoises*, *Cows*, *Cats*, and *How Do Tornadoes Form?*. She is also a published playwright. Her plays have been produced in schools and community theaters across the country.